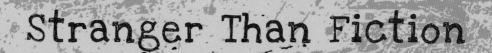

Stranger Than Fiction

STRANGE MEDICINE

By Virginia Loh-Hagan

Disclaimer: This series focuses on the strangest of the strange. Have fun reading about strange people and things! But please do not try any of the antics in this book. Be safe and smart!

45th Parallel Press

Published in the United States of America by Cherry Lake Publishing
Ann Arbor, Michigan
www.cherrylakepublishing.com

Reading Adviser: Marla Conn MS, Ed., Literacy specialist, Read-Ability, Inc.
Book Designer: Melinda Millward

Photo Credits: © Kotin/Shutterstock.com, cover, 7; © Andrey_Popov/Shutterstock.com, 1; © SERGEI PRIMAKOV/Shutterstock.com, 5; © fotohunter/Shutterstock.com, 6; © Juri Pozzi/Shutterstock.com, 8; © Sanit Fuangnakhon/Shutterstock.com, 10; © LTim/Shutterstock.com, 11; © Wesley Fryer/http://www.flickr.com/ CC-BY-2.0, 12; © Ymri Wilt/DanitaDelimont.com "Danita Delimont Photography"/Newscom, 13; © MasterQ/Shutterstock.com, 14; © sdigital/iStockphoto, 15; © Semen Lixodeev/Shutterstock.com, 16; © funnyangel/Shutterstock.com, 18; © EyePress News EyePress/Newscom, 19; © kzww/Shutterstock.com, 20; © duncan1890/iStockphoto, 21; © Mirko Sobotta/Shutterstock.com, 22; © Zadiraka Evgenii/Shutterstock.com, 23; © viti/iStockphoto, 24; © KarenMower/iStockphoto, 25; © Bucchi Francesco/Shutterstock.com, 26; © Alfredo Cerra/Shutterstock.com, 27; © Masson/Shutterstock.com, 28; © Roberto Castillo/Shutterstock.com, 30; © pepmiba/iStockphoto, 31

Graphic Element Credits: ©saki80/Shutterstock.com, back cover, front cover, multiple interior pages; ©queezz/Shutterstock.com, back cover, front cover, multiple interior pages; ©Ursa Major/Shutterstock.com, front cover, multiple interior pages; ©Zilu8/Shutterstock.com, multiple interior pages

45th Parallel Press is an imprint of Cherry Lake Publishing.

Library of Congress Cataloging-in-Publication Data

Names: Loh-Hagan, Virginia, author.
Title: Strange medicine / by Virginia Loh-Hagan.
Description: Ann Arbor, MI : Cherry Lake Publishing, [2017] | Series: Stranger than fiction
Identifiers: LCCN 2017001053| ISBN 9781634728904 (hardcover) | ISBN 9781534100688 (pbk.) |
    ISBN 9781634729796 (pdf) | ISBN 9781534101579 (hosted ebook)
Subjects: LCSH: Traditional medicine—Juvenile literature. | Alternative medicine—Juvenile literature. |
    Medicine—History—Juvenile literature.
Classification: LCC GR880 .L64 2017 | DDC 615.8/8—dc23
LC record available at https://lccn.loc.gov/2017001053

Printed in the United States of America
Corporate Graphics

About the Author

Dr. Virginia Loh-Hagan is an author, university professor, former classroom teacher, and curriculum designer. She believes drinking green tea will keep her alive forever. She lives in San Diego with her very tall husband and very naughty dogs. To learn more about her, visit www.virginialoh.com.

Table of Contents

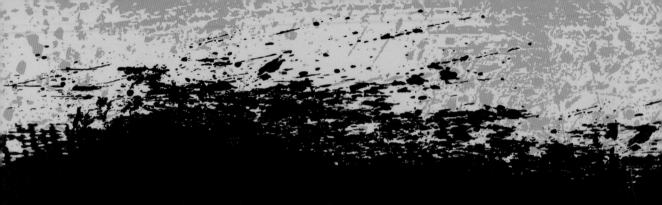

Introduction

People get older. They get sick. They need medicine. They need treatment. They need doctors. Some people will do anything to get well. People have different ways of solving health problems.

Medicine is a science. Doctors learn new things all the time. They test. They research. They try things out. They make mistakes. They use what they know at the time. They learn more. They get smarter. They get better.

There are many strange ways to treat sicknesses. They're so strange that they're hard to believe. They sound like fiction. But these stories are all true!

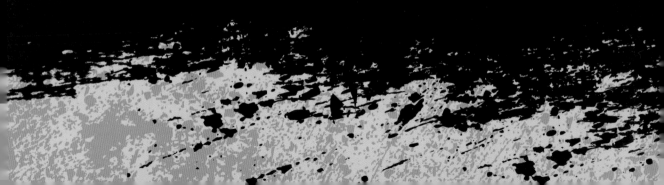

Many cultures have healers. These
are people who help cure illness.

chapter one

Needles

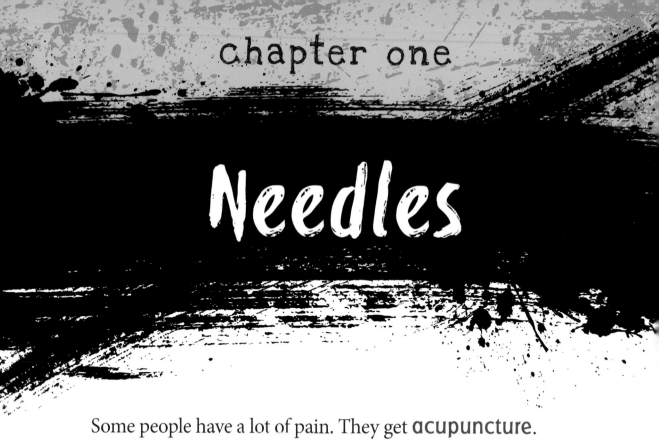

Some people have a lot of pain. They get **acupuncture**. Acupuncture comes from China. Acupuncturists see the body as an energy field. Acupuncture balances that energy. It **stimulates** nerves, muscles, and tissues. Stimulate means to excite.

The **chi** is a person's life force. It flows through the body. It flows through 12 organs. It flows through 12 **meridians**. Meridians are points in the body. The points are all connected.

Acupuncturists use needles to move chi. Needles come in different types and sizes.

Some people won't take drugs. They don't want operations. Acupuncture is an option.

There's a different needle for specific body parts and problems.

People lie down on a padded table. Acupuncturists clean the area. They insert needles into meridians. They tap, twirl, or jiggle each needle. They insert some needles deeper than others. Sometimes, they heat the needles. Sometimes, they burn a dried herb. It gives off a little smoke and a good smell. Sometimes, they send electricity through the needles. This stimulates points that needles can't reach.

Once all the needles are inserted, people rest. Some people fall asleep. Sessions last 15 to 60 minutes. Acupuncturists remove the needles.

Dirty needles spread sicknesses.

Explained by Science

Being sick is no fun. Bad germs enter the body. They enter through the air we breathe. They enter through the food we eat. Coughing spreads sickness. People cough into their hands. They touch things. Other people touch the same things. They get sick. Bad germs hide in the body's healthy cells. They change. They trick our bodies. They infect cells. The body sends blood and cells to these areas. Cells fight the sick germs. Bodies begin to heal. A stuffy nose is a good sign. Mucus protects the body. It traps the bad germs. Blowing the nose pushes them out.

chapter two

Snail Slime

Snails make slime. People use this slime. Ancient Greeks used it to heal skin wounds. Early doctors made snail **syrup**. Syrup is a thick juice. People found snails. They took off their shells. They slit the snails' bodies. They put them in a bag. They added sugar. They hung the bag. Slime came out. People ate this slime. They thought it cured sore throats. They thought it cured coughs.

Some people pricked a snail. Slime oozed out. People put it in their ear. They thought this cured earaches.

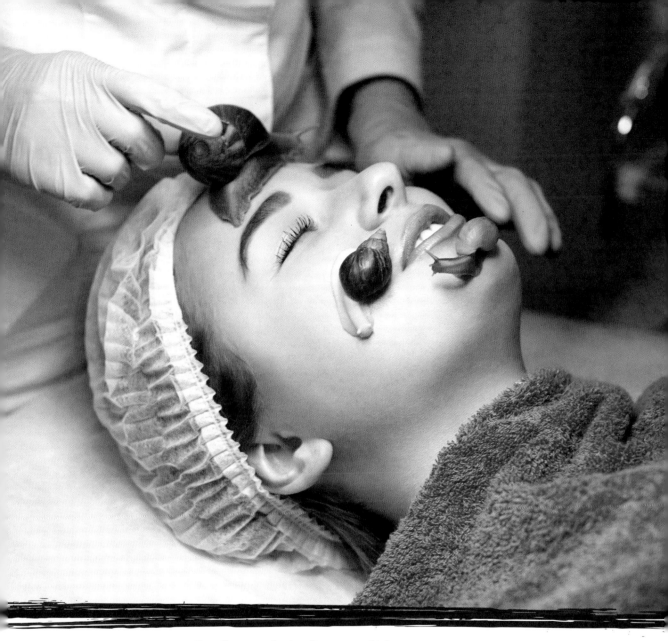

Snails use their slime to glide, or move.

Today, people use snail slime to enhance beauty. Women put it on their faces. They hide wrinkles. They cover spots. They cover scars.

chapter three

Snake Oil

Chinese water snakes have oil. The oil is rich in good fats. Chinese healers used it to ease **joint** pain. Joints are body parts that move. Examples are knees and wrists.

Chinese workers helped build U.S. railroads. They did this in the 1800s. This was hard work. It caused back pain. The Chinese workers rubbed snake oil on their joints. They shared it with other workers.

Some people thought they could make money. They sold "snake oil." But they used different snakes. This snake oil

The fake snake oil was probably from rattlesnakes.

didn't really help. Sellers tricked people. Their snake oil was fake.

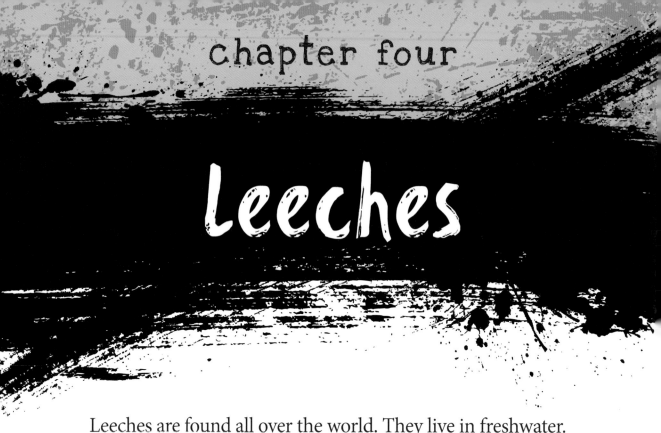

chapter four

Leeches

Leeches are found all over the world. They live in freshwater. They feed on blood. They bite living things. They suck out the blood. They have special spit. Their spit increases blood flow. It prevents **clotting**. Clotting is the stopping of blood flow. Victims can bleed for hours. This lets new blood enter the wound area. Veins regrow. Veins regain flow.

Sometimes, leeches cause problems. They slip off. They attach to unwanted places. They also fall off when done eating. They become **engorged** with blood. Engorged means swollen. Their victims can suffer from blood loss.

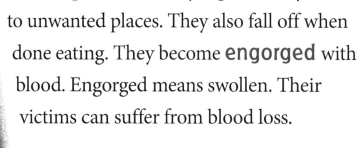

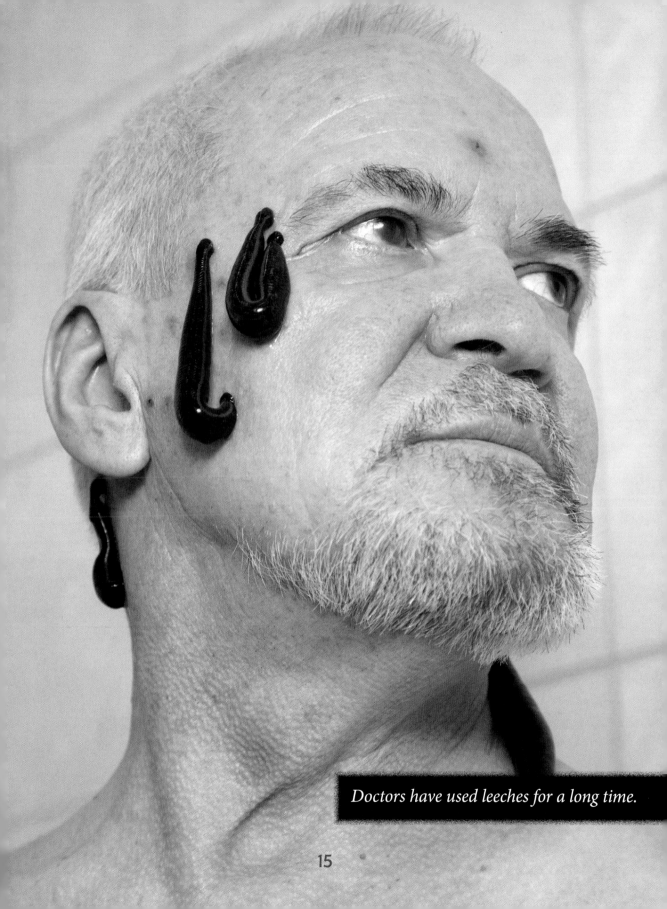

Doctors have used leeches for a long time.

Egyptians used leeches 5,000 years ago. They put leeches on sick people. Leeches sipped out the "bad blood." They restored the body's balance. This was called **bloodletting**. People thought leeches cured everything.

Today, doctors use leeches in surgery. Leeches draw blood to damaged tissues. This lets doctors work on body parts. An example is ears. Ears have tiny veins. Their veins clot. Leeches help. They keep the blood flowing. They've saved lives and limbs.

Some people created leech farms.

Spotlight Biography

Elizabeth Blackwell was the first woman doctor in the United States. She was the first woman to get a medical degree. But it wasn't easy. She applied to many medical schools. She got rejected. Geneva Medical College accepted her. But the college admitted her as a joke. The college wasn't sure about a woman doctor. The college's leader let the students vote. There were 150 men who voted. If one of them voted no, Blackwell wouldn't be let in. The students thought Blackwell was a joke. They voted yes. They didn't think she'd last long. Blackwell surprised them. She graduated two years later in 1849. She opened a medical school for women.

chapter five

Bee Stings

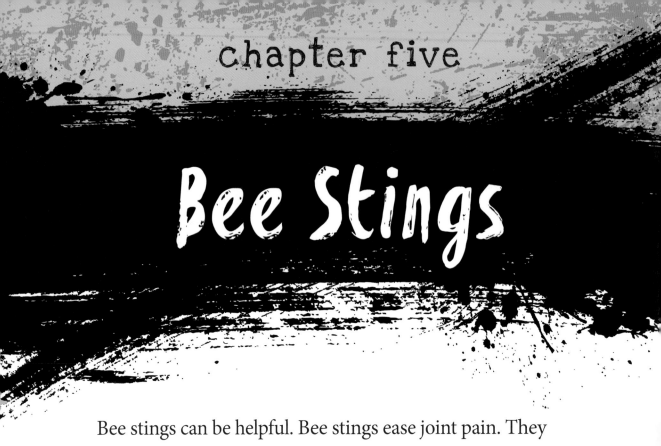

Bee stings can be helpful. Bee stings ease joint pain. They ease nerve pain. They speed up the healing process. They ease muscle weakness.

Some doctors use bee **venom**. Venom is poison that is injected. The doctors put the venom in needles. They inject people. Other doctors use a live bee. They hold it with tweezers. They put it near the skin. They force it to sting people. Some people get stung about 80 times a day.

Ancient Egyptians used bee stings.

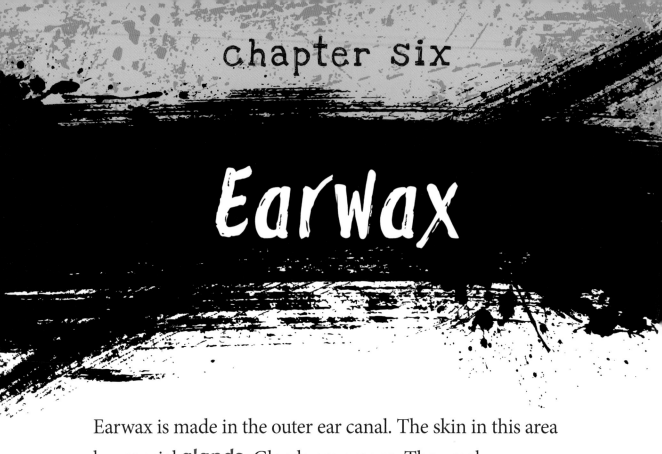

chapter six

Earwax

Earwax is made in the outer ear canal. The skin in this area has special **glands**. Glands are organs. They make earwax. Earwax moves to the ear opening. It falls out. Or it's removed when people wash their hair.

Earwax protects the ear. It makes sure ears don't get dry and itchy. It fights off infections. It shields the eardrums. It traps dirt and dust.

Some doctors used earwax. They mixed earwax with mud. They used this to treat headaches. Some doctors used earwax to

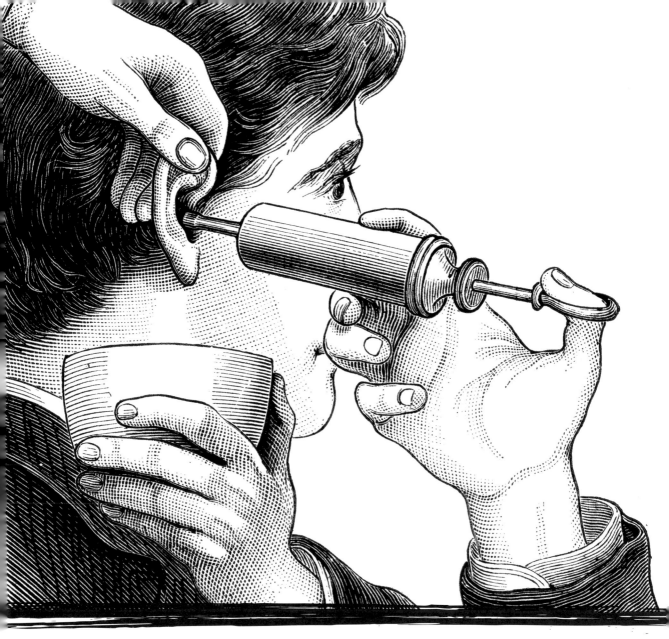

Earwax is also called cerumen.

fix chapped lips. The first lip balm may have been earwax. Some doctors used earwax to cover cuts and cold sores.

chapter seven

Dead Mouse Paste

Ancient Egyptians ate a lot of sand. Sand got into their food. Sand is gritty. It wore down their teeth. This caused toothaches. Egyptians wanted a cure. They used dead or rotting mice. They mashed the mice. They made a paste. They put it on the toothache. Sometimes, they'd stick a dead mouse in their mouths.

In England, people also used mice. They cut mice in half. They put the bloody part on warts. This happened during Queen Elizabeth's time.

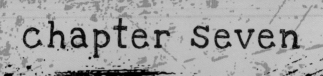

Mice have been used in other cures. Some people cooked mice in oil. They used this

22

There's no science for using mice in cures.

to stop gray hair. Some people roasted mice into ashes.
They combined ashes with milk. They used this to cure
whooping cough.

chapter eight

Maggots

Maggots are fly **larvae**. Larvae are like worms. They're the stage between eggs and flies. Blowfly maggots are used to treat wounds.

Maggots make special spit. The spit eats dead tissue. It leaves healthy tissue alone. Maggots clean wounds. They kill the bad germs. This speeds up healing.

Maggots were useful during wars. Military doctors used maggots. Soldiers got hurt. They needed quick help. Doctors put maggots on wounds. Maggots helped keep infection away. Maggots saved lives.

24

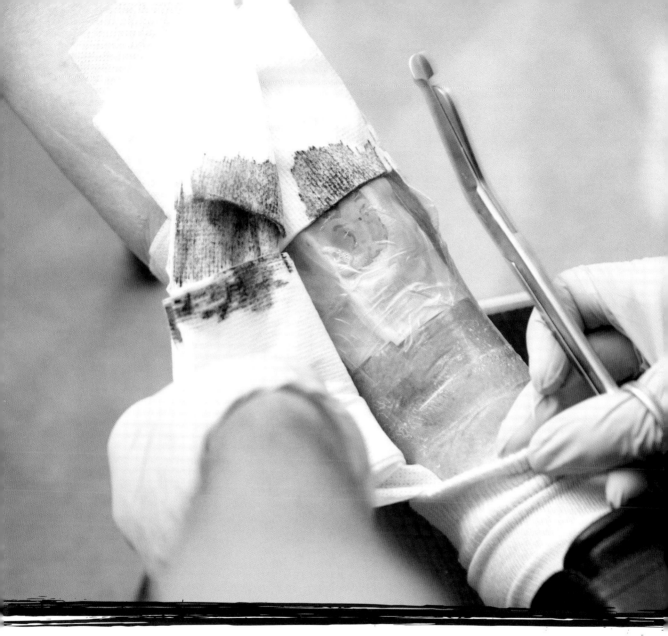

Maggots need wet wounds.

Today's doctors still use maggots. They put maggots in a bag. The bag is like a tea bag. It keeps maggots from crawling away. It keeps them from growing into flies.

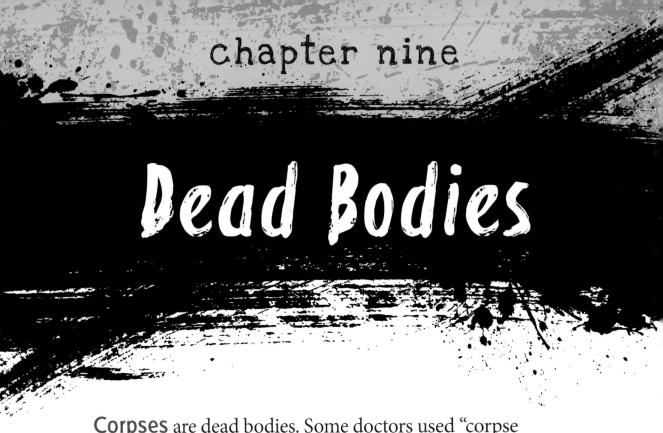

chapter nine

Dead Bodies

Corpses are dead bodies. Some doctors used "corpse medicine." They mixed human flesh, blood, or bone. They thought these medicines were magical. They thought people took in the power of the corpses' spirits.

Ancient Romans drank the blood of dead warriors. They thought it cured sicknesses. They thought it'd make them stronger.

Some doctors used "mummy powder." This happened in the 12th century. Mummies were stolen from graves. These doctors ground them up. They made powder.

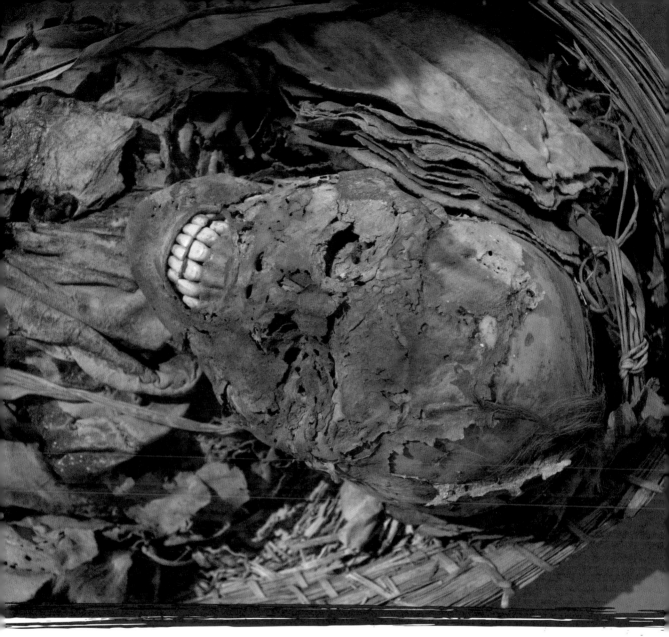

People thought eating skulls would cure headaches.

They mixed it with other things. They fed it to sick people. They put in on wounds. They thought this cured all kinds of things.

Some German doctors used human fat. They rubbed human fat into skin. They did this to cure joint pain.

King Charles II was English. He ruled in the 17th century. He drank King's Drops. It was a drink. It was made with crumbled human skull.

In the 17th century, people got in sword fights. They got wounded. Doctors used the Powder of **Sympathy**. Sympathy means caring for another. Doctors mixed earthworms, pig brains, rust, and mummies. They made a powder. They put the powder on the weapon that had caused the injury. This was supposed to help cure the injury. It didn't work.

Using dead bodies as a cure didn't work.

Try This!

- Spend time outside. Go for a walk. Enjoy the sunshine. You'll get vitamin D. You'll get exercise.

- Drink ginger tea. It eases stomachaches.

- Grow aloe plants. Aloe eases burns.

- Visit your doctor. Get a check-up every year.

- Eat radishes. You'll feel less stuffed up.

- Make oatmeal. Put it on skin rashes.

- For hiccups: Get a teaspoon of sugar. Put it under your tongue. Swallow the sugar.

- Eat an apple a day. Keep the doctor away! Make sure to eat the skin. The skin is the healthiest part. Apples are full of fiber. They're full of vitamins. They'll keep you healthy.

chapter ten

Farts

The Black Death was deadly. It killed many people. It happened in the 1300s. It happened in Europe, Asia, and North Africa. People died within a few days. They had fevers. They had bleeding from their lungs. They threw up a lot. They had **boils**. Boils are painful skin bumps.

People wanted cures. They believed anything. Doctors thought the Black Death was caused by deadly **vapors**. Vapors are gases. People thought the sickness was **airborne**. Airborne means carried by the air. Doctors thought people got sick from breathing the air. They thought good vapors could stop the Black Death. Doctors stored farts in

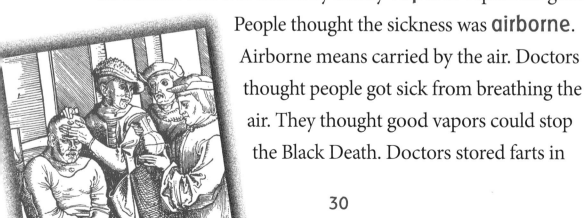

30

These stinky jars did not work.

jars. They told people to smell the jars. They thought this would keep them safe.

Consider This!

Take a Position! Doctors prescribe medicine. They think medicines help sick people. Some people don't like taking medicines. Do you think medicine is helpful or harmful? Argue your point with reasons and evidence.

Say What? Research a disease. A disease is a sickness. Explain the symptoms. Symptoms are signs of sickness. Explain the treatment.

Think About It! When you're sick, do your parents make you chicken soup? Why do you think they do that? Chicken soup is believed to make people feel better. Research this and learn more. Find out if it's true or not.

Learn More!

- *Medicine: The Definitive Illustrated History.* New York: Dorling Kindersley Publishing, 2016.
- Raum, Elizabeth. *The Cold, Hard Facts About Science and Medicine in Colonial America.* Mankato, MN: Capstone Press, 2012.
- Ward, Brian. *The History of Medicine: Healthcare Around the World and Through the Ages.* San Francisco: Armadillo, 2016.

Glossary

acupuncture (AK-yoo-pungk-chur) Eastern medicine practice that involves inserting needles in special body points to balance energy

airborne (AIR-born) carried by the air

bloodletting (BLUHD-let-ing) the practice of removing "bad blood" to increase health

boils (BOYLZ) painful skin bumps filled with pus

chi (CHEE) a person's life force

clotting (KLAHT-ing) stopping the flow of blood

corpses (KORPS-iz) dead bodies

engorged (en-GORJD) swollen

glands (GLANDZ) organs

joint (JOYNT) body part that moves, like knees or wrists

larvae (LAHR-vee) worm stage of life between eggs and flies

maggots (MAG-uhts) worm stage of life between eggs and flies

meridians (muh-RID-ee-uhnz) points in the body

stimulates (STIM-yuh-lates) excites

sympathy (SIM-puh-thee) caring for another

syrup (SIR-uhp) a thick liquid or juice

vapors (VAY-purz) gases

venom (VEN-uhm) poison that is injected under the skin

Index